LIZARDS FOR BEG...

PREFACE

I have had an almost fanatical interest in lizards ever since I was a small child. Pictures of exotic species conjured up visions of giant dinosaurs roaming the plains or of ferocious dragons on the hunt for human prey. Most modern lizards, however, are totally harmless to human beings, and none of them really go out of their way to eat us!

As a child I captured and kept the little common lizards, *Lacerta vivipara,* of my native England and was fascinated by their apparently endless appetite as they devoured the numerous little spiders and insects I fed to them. Later I graduated to more exotic species from southern Europe, Africa, and North America, many of which could be obtained in pet shops or from specialist importers. Eventually I became a reptile curator in a zoological park, where I gained experience with a great number of species from many parts of the world.

During the past couple of decades those who practice lizard keeping as a hobby have increased dramatically in numbers. New enthusiasts are continually joining the hobby, and there is an escalating quest for new facts about the biology and care of these fascinating reptiles. Students of zoology are increasingly turning to herpetology in their curricula, and studies on the ecology and behavior of lizards in the wild are producing many interesting and astonishing facts. At the same time, while taxonomists continue to revise the classification of known species, new species are still being discovered and described sporadically. Indeed, a new species of skink, which has even been relegated to a new genus, recently was discovered just 40 miles away from my home in Australia.

This work is intended to be a small but concise guide to lizard keeping as a hobby, and I have endeavored to include all of the information that the beginner to lizard keeping will require to set him off on the right footing for a long and fascinating affair with these charming creatures.

Green Anoles, *Anolis carolinensis,* are small and hardy insectivores. One would make an excellent first pet lizard. Photo by Isabelle Francais

SOME LIZARD NATURAL HISTORY

Lizards form the zoological suborder Lacertilia and share with snakes (suborder Serpentes) the order Squamata, which is contained in the class Reptilia. Being reptiles, lizards have characteristics that make them different from other classes of vertebrates such as fishes, amphibians, birds, and mammals. Some typical characteristics of reptiles are that they have a dry, scaly skin; respire with lungs; and are ectothermic (cold-blooded). No other class of vertebrate (backboned) animals has all of these attributes. Fish may have scales and be ectothermic, but they don't have lungs. Amphibians may be ectothermic and have lungs, but they don't have a scaly skin; while birds and mammals both are endothermic (warm-blooded).

Different species of lizards form more than one half of the total species of recent reptiles, and over 3,700 species are recognized. They range in size from the tiny, rare Virgin Gorda Gecko, *Sphaerodactylus parthenopion*, which reaches a maximum length (including tail) of 3.8 cm (1.5 in), to the massive Komodo Dragon,

Amblyrhynchus cristatus, the Marine Iguana, lives in colonies on the Galapagos Islands. They are legally protected and never available to the hobbyist. Photo by Karl H. Switak

Smile! Not really. This is the defensive display of a Tokay Gecko, *Gekko gecko*. Photo by Karl H. Switak

Varanus komodoensis, with a recorded length of 3.1 m (10 ft 2 in). This record specimen was exhibited in the St. Louis Zoological Gardens, Missouri, during 1937, at which time it weighed 166 kg (365 lb)! The vast majority of lizard species, however, are confined to a length range of 15-45 cm (6-18 in).

Lizards occur in suitable climates on every continent except Antarctica. They are found in habitats ranging from deserts to rainforests, and from prairies to mountain ranges. Although the greatest number of species occur in the tropics and subtropics, some are found as far north as southern Canada and as far south as Tierra del Fuego at the tip of South America. In Europe, the Viviparous Lizard, *Lacerta vivipara*, extends to some areas within the Arctic Circle. A few species are littoral (inhabiting the seashore), while others are semiaquatic in freshwater. A single species, the Marine Iguana, *Amblyrhynchus cristatus*, of the Galapagos Islands, actually forages below sea level for its staple diet of seaweed!

A typical lizard has an elongated body and a long, tapering tail. It has four limbs, each furnished with five digits. However, there are many variations from the typical; some have reductions in the number of digits, others have reduced or vestigial limbs or even no visible limbs at all. There are other species with short fat tails instead of long tapering ones.

One distinctive feature of lizards and other reptiles is the horny skin that is folded into

Another typical feature of many lizard species is the ability to shed all or part of the tail. Some shed the tail readily and voluntarily, others less readily only when the tail is seized by a predator. The tail is shed by a process known as autotomy, and the break occurs across a weak spot (the fracture plane) across one of the tail

This male South American anole, *Anolis fuscoauratus*, has extended his brightly colored dewlap. This indicates he is defending his territory or wooing a potential mate.Photo by Paul Freed

scales. Different species have varying types of scales; some are large and plate-like, others are tiny and granular. Scales may overlap or may be juxtaposed. They may be smooth and glossy in some species, rough and keeled in others. In some lizards, many of the scales are modified into protective spines.

vertebrae. Tail shedding is a protective mechanism that keeps a predator occupied with the wriggling appendage while the main body of the animal quickly makes its escape. A new but less spectacular tail will eventually grow in place of the shed one. Another feature of the tail in some lizards, especially chamaeleons

The Veiled Chameleon, *Chamaeleo calyptratus*, is a beautiful but demanding captive. Photo by Zoltan Takacs

and Prehensile-tailed Skinks, *Corucia zebrata*, is prehensility. The tail, in effect, acts as a fifth limb, allowing the reptiles to grip twigs and branches and giving them more stability.

While most lizards are carnivorous (meat eaters), preying on invertebrate and vertebrate animals of suitable size, some are omnivorous, feeding on a mixture of animal and vegetable foods, and a few are quite herbivorous, feeding mostly on vegetation.

An important reptilian feature of lizards that has a bearing on the way we keep them is the fact that they are ectothermic or cold-blooded. This means that unlike birds and mammals, lizards are unable to maintain a constant optimum body temperature through metabolism; they have to rely on external temperatures through a process known as behavioral thermoregulation. In the morning a lizard will emerge from its overnight refuge and bask in the sun until it reaches an optimum operating temperature. It then goes off to seek food or indulge in mating activities before seeking out a shady, cooler spot where it can cool down somewhat. By moving from warmer to cooler spots throughout the day, the lizard can maintain a surprisingly constant temperature. It instinctively knows its optimum temperature requirement and actively regulates it. In cooler temperate regions, lizards remain inactive, often through several months of hibernation, until temperatures are again high enough for them to function efficiently. It is only in tropical areas that lizards may be active throughout the year, and even there they may enter into estivation during periods of drought. It is in tropical regions that the majority of nocturnal lizards live, especially geckos.

A close-up view of the beautiful dorsal crest of a male Green Basilisk, *Basiliscus plumifrons*. In the female, the crest is greatly reduced. Photo by David J. Zoffer

HOUSING FOR PET LIZARDS

The type of housing you will use for your pet lizards will depend on the size of the species you intend to keep and its ecological requirements. You should always have the accommodations ready to use before you acquire any lizards. It is a mistake to obtain specimens first and then have to worry about how you are going to house them. In this and the following chapter we will be discussing types of housing for pet lizards and the life support systems that will provide the correct environmental requirements for a range of species.

THE GLASS TERRARIUM

A simple glass aquarium tank of the type sold for fish keeping is ideal as a starter terrarium and can be used for many species. Most modern aquarium tanks are constructed from glass sheets cemented together with special silicone adhesive. Such aquaria can be purchased at any pet shop and come in various sizes. You can have a terrarium constructed to order, specifying the shape and dimensions of the tank to your own special needs (perhaps you have some corner or alcove in the house where you need a terrarium of specific design) and to the

A Collared Lizard, *Crotaphytus collaris*. This species requires a large, arid terrarium to thrive. Photo by Aaron Norman

This juvenile Nile Monitor, *Varanus niloticus,* can grow to a length of 6 feet or more. Its size and aggressive disposition make this a poor choice for the beginner. Photo by R. D. Bartlett

needs of the species you are going to keep. Terrestrial lizards, for example, will need a relatively low, flat construction with a large floor area, while arboreal species require a tall tank with room to affix vertical branches and tall plants.

The lid of the terrarium can be made from a piece of thick, heavy plywood or sheet aluminum with two large holes (one at each end) covered with fine wire gauze, for ventilation purposes. Cut the lid to size so that it just rests on the strengthening strips just inside the top of the tank. A small handle affixed to the lid will make it easy to lift off when necessary. As many lizard species are talented escape artists, ensure that there are no gaps wider than 3 mm (0.12 in). A much simpler

and usually satisfactory alternative is to purchase a standard lid at your pet shop. These usually consist of a metal or plastic frame fitted with mesh or wire screening of various sizes. In some lids the screened portion is attached so it can be slid out rather than lifted off, an excellent way to help prevent escapes.

Terraria can, of course, be constructed from a range of other materials, including wood, metal, fiberglass, and so on. I have seen some excellent lizard cages improvised from such items as old TV cabinets and shop display cabinets. Many specialist dealers today make custom terraria that range from large rainforest enclosures complete with humidifiers to shelf units designed to hold the shoe boxes

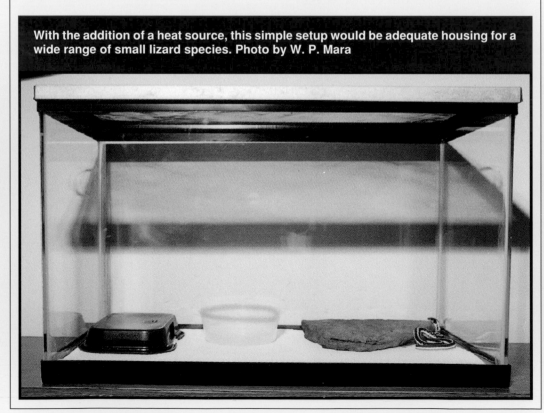

With the addition of a heat source, this simple setup would be adequate housing for a wide range of small lizard species. Photo by W. P. Mara

This outdoor enclosure with live plants is ideal for arboreal lizards such as chameleons and day geckos. Photo by R. D. Bartlett.

and sweater boxes in which many lizards are bred commercially. The main requirements are that terraria must be escape-proof and able to resist humidity in the case of rainforest displays. When using wood, it is best to preserve it with a coating of water-resistant varnish, paint, or fiberglass resin, being sure that all residues and volatile components have plenty of time to totally disperse.

CAGE FURNISHINGS

Substrate Materials

Simple breeding or rearing cages are best floored with newspaper or paper towels. These are absorbent and easy to change frequently. For the display terrarium a substrate of gravel, leaf litter, bark chippings, or similar materials is suitable. A recent innovation is terrarium carpeting, a floor covering produced by several companies. Such floor coverings are attractive, mildew resistant, and washable. Less suitable substitutes include synthetic grass carpeting or even old bath towels. Whatever kind of flooring is used, it is important that it is cleaned and sterilized regularly. It is a good idea to have spare floor coverings ready to replace those that are being cleaned.

Rocks

These provide a natural looking backdrop for species from desert

Sand works well as a substrate for desert-dwelling lizards such as these Leopard Geckos, *Eublepharis macularius.* Note the inclusion of a heat source, water bowl, and shelter. Photo by Isabelle Francais

An artificial cow skull, cactus, and cholla wood enrich this Leopard Gecko enclosure. Photo by Jerry R. Loll

or rocky areas and will supply locations on which they can bask. You can purchase suitable rocks in pet shops, including those made of Styrofoam or papier mache to reduce weight. Rocks can be piled up to create caves and crevices that your lizards will use as refuges, but be sure they are fixed securely to avoid accidents; silicone cements work well. You can collect your own rocks, but be sure they are thoroughly cleaned and dried before you use them.

Tree Branches

Climbing lizards will require branches and twigs on which to practice their skills, as well as to bask. Dead wood is preferable to branches recently cut from living trees, some of which may emit poisonous saps. Driftwood from river banks or from the sea shore is ideal as it will have been exposed to the elements, will be attractively sun bleached, and usually is relatively smooth; be sure to thoroughly soak all driftwood to remove salt, silt, and dead plants and animals. Branches should be fixed securely in the cage so that they are unable to topple. A climbing branch that ends directly at the surface of the terrarium might be an excellent escape route for an active lizard, so it might be best to be sure all branches are fixed at least a few centimeters below the rim.

Plants

There is no doubt that a display of healthy plants in the terrarium adds an esthetic charm that is hard to beat. Rainforest terraria in particular should have a few living plants. It is best to retain living plants in their pots. These can be arranged in the terrarium and the pots concealed with rocks or bits of cork bark. Many plant species of the type commonly marketed as "house plants" are suitable for the humid terrarium. Cacti and succulents may be suitable for drier terraria. It always is best to keep a spare set of plants so that you can change them at intervals while the stressed plants relax in sunshine for a month or so. Unfortunately, there is not much point in trying to grow plants along with large, boisterous lizards, especially herbivorous species. In such cases artificial plants can be used effectively.

This Koch's Day Gecko, *Phelsuma madagascariensis kochi,* basks on a bamboo perch. This arboreal species fares well in a tall, well-planted terrarium. Photo by R. D. Bartlett.

LIFE SUPPORT SYSTEMS

Lizards kept in captivity must be provided with environmental conditions that are as near as possible to those of their native habitats. As it usually is impossible to mimic natural conditions in the enclosed terrarium, we have to use compromise systems in order to reproduce an optimum environment.

TEMPERATURE

Being ectothermic (cold-blooded), lizards are unable to maintain their body temperatures at a relatively constant level without the assistance of an external heat source. In nature, the natural heat sources mainly come directly or indirectly from the sun. By the process of thermoregulation, lizards

Access to the proper range of temperatures is essential to successful lizard keeping. This Australian skink, *Egernia hosmeri*, prefers temperatures between 80 and 100 degrees Fahrenheit. Photo by R. W. VanDevender

The climatic constituents that we have to take into consideration are temperature, lighting and photoperiod, ventilation, and humidity. Modern technology now enables us to produce optimum conditions for habitats ranging from arid deserts to tropical rain forests.

maintain an optimum body temperature by basking directly in the sun and/or by coming into contact with sun-warmed surfaces. Unless we keep our lizards in open-air enclosures, it is usually quite impossible to use natural sunlight as a source of heat. Sunlight through the glass of a terrarium will be magnified, and the terrarium will overheat dramatically in a short space of time. Many a novice lizard keeper has lost his pets through placing their terrarium in direct sunlight. Electrical heating of one form or another is the answer to this problem.

Incandescent Bulbs

The simplest method of terrarium heating, and one that has been in use since the pioneering days of terrarium keeping, is the ordinary domestic incandescent (tungsten) light bulb. Bulbs come in various sizes (wattages), and one or more can be used to maintain suitable temperatures in terraria of most sizes. Unfortunately the quality of light emitted by such bulbs is inadequate for the requirements of most diurnal basking lizards, so they must be used in conjunction with other light sources. Recently some manufacturers have produced specially coated bulbs that mimic at least some of the wavelengths of light necessary for healthy lizards. Other special coatings provide heat with little or no light, useful when warming nocturnally active lizards. A bulb used for heating can be installed in the terrarium lid, and the required temperature can be maintained by experimenting with a thermometer and various wattages, or by use of a thermostat. It usually is prudent to mount the bulb in a socket that is contained within a reflective shade so that most of the heat is directed onto a basking surface below the lamp. The temperature of the basking area can be adjusted by raising or lowering the lamp.

Because all incandescent bulbs can cause horrendous burns if a lizard should gain access to them, all bulbs must be securely mounted above the terrarium lid with strong screening below so no lizard can get close to them.

A more up to date version of the tungsten bulb is the spotlight that has its own built-in reflector. They can be used in much the same way as the normal bulbs. Infra-red bulbs that emit either white or red light also often are used specifically to warm up basking areas. A disadvantage of light-emitting bulbs used for heating is that they emit light continuously, even at night when it is not required. This can be overcome to some extent by using a dark colored (red or blue) bulb at night. As the night temperature usually must be cooler than that of the day, the colored bulb should be of a lower wattage than the day bulb. For example, a 100 watt bulb normally will provide adequate daytime heating for a small terrarium with dimensions of 60 x 30 x 30 cm (approx. 24 x 12 x 12 in) and a 25 watt colored bulb will suffice for the night.

Heating Pads, Tapes, and Cables

A number of electrical heating devices specially manufactured for terraria are available. Heating pads may be placed below terraria or can be used against one of the sides. Cables may be useful for placing in a gravel substrate, while tapes can be affixed along the bottom edges of the terrarium. Heating tapes usually require that they be cut to fit the terrarium and then wired into the main circuits; if you are unsure as to how to set up tapes, for safety consult an electrician.

devices should be used specifically to the manufacturer's instructions. They must never get wet while plugged in, should always be kept clean, and must be carefully watched for hot spots. In the case of lizards that thermoregulate by basking in sunlight from above (Green

Banded geckos, like this *Coleonyx mitratus* hatchling, are occasionally offered for sale. They need a hot and fairly dry environment. Photo by R. D. Bartlett

Heated Rocks

The most recent special heating innovations for terraria are so called "hot rocks," artificial pieces of rock (usually made from plaster of Paris or a plastic resin) containing a heating element that may or may not be controlled thermostatically. Needless to say, the thermostatically controlled rocks are more efficient. All commercially produced heating

Iguanas, etc.), the pineal eye on top of the skull keeps track of how much basking time is necessary for the lizard; heat from below, especially directly against the belly, may not register and the lizard may not be able to sense the fact that it is burning. Hot rocks have led to bad ventral burns in some lizards when not accompanied by overhead basking lights.

Veiled Chameleons, *Chamaeleo calyptratus*, need to be kept in cages that are warm, moist, and furnished with plenty of climbing branches. This is a gravid female. Photo by R. D. Bartlett

Aquarium Heaters

Tubular glass aquarium heaters, with or without a thermostat, may have their uses in the lizard terrarium, especially for species that need high humidity. In the aquaterrarium, the aquarium heater simply can be placed in the water area and used just as you would use it in an aquarium for tropical fish. Alternatively, where a large body of water is not required, the aquarium heater can be placed in a tall jar of water that can be concealed in a corner of the terrarium. The heater cable should be passed through a perforated lid fixed over the jar to prevent lizards from gaining access and accidentally drowning. Some aquarium heaters can be used out of water and can be placed inside a hollowed out log, a clay pipe, or an artificial hollow rock. Most common aquarium heaters, however, will malfunction if turned on when dry.

Temperature Gradation

As lizards have a preferred optimum temperature, it is dangerous to expose them to a constant high temperature without facilities to cool off. A temperature gradation in the terrarium will allow the reptiles to move from warmer to cooler parts of the substrate and vice versa. This can be achieved by placing the heating apparatus at only one end of the terrarium. The main basking area will be close to the heat source, temperatures becoming progressively less toward the other end of the cage. When using a thermostat it is best to place the sensor in the center of the terrarium and set it to an average temperature. If, for example, you want the temperature to be 30°C (86°F) at the "hot" end and 24°C (75°F) at the cold end, you could try setting the thermostat at 27°C (81°F). You may have to experiment using a thermometer before you get it right.

Night Temperature

Night temperatures often are lower than those prevailing during the day. The differences between day and night temperatures may be as much as 15°C (about 30°F) for species from temperate, subtropical, and tropical montane regions to as little as 4°C (about 8°F) for species from lowland equatorial regions. For many species the heating apparatus can be simply switched off at night; the room temperature in most dwellings is adequate overnight. Should higher nighttime temperatures be required, it may be necessary to have a double thermostat system, one for daytime, the other for nighttime.

Seasonal Temperature

Seasonal temperature changes should also be provided where necessary. Species from temperate and subtropical regions are especially influenced by seasonal temperature changes as well as photoperiod. While winter temperatures in some natural habitats may descend to below the freezing point, lizards from such areas know where to hibernate to avoid sub-zero temperatures. (Of course, the terrarium would have to provide sufficiently deep substrates to allow them to burrow to a warm level.) It would be dangerous in the terrarium to copy such winter climates, and a compromise reduction of temperature for a shorter period is adequate. A winter reduction of 10°C (about 20°F) usually is satisfactory.

LIGHTING

Lighting goes hand in hand with heating. Many lizard species require natural sunlight to remain in the best of health. The ultraviolet rays help stimulate the manufacture of essential vitamin D3, a deficiency that will cause various metabolic problems that could, over a period of time, even be fatal. Fortunately we now have forms of artificial lighting of a quality that is a good substitute for sunlight. Most such lights come in the form of fluorescent tubes that provide broad-spectrum lighting coming close to the necessary wavelengths of sunlight.

While incandescent bulbs used for heating will provide incidental supplementary light, they must be used in conjunction with broad-spectrum lamps for many diurnal basking species, especially those from temperate and subtropical regions.

Nocturnal lizards such as many geckos are less dependent on sunlight or its substitute, though it will do no harm to include broad-spectrum lighting in any setup.

Seasonal changes in photoperiod (hours of daylight) also are important, especially if we want our lizards to reproduce. We know that photoperiod decreases in the winter and increases in the summer. The seasonal changes in photoperiod are progressively greater from the Equator to the poles. In temperate regions the period of daylight can be as much as 16 hours in the summer and as little as eight hours in the winter. By knowing the latitude of your lizard species' natural habitat you will be able to work out the photoperiod requirements in the terrarium. Equatorial species of course require 12-hour photoperiods the year around, though even these may be stimulated to breed with a small reduction at the right time.

VENTILATION AND HUMIDITY

While adequate ventilation in the terrarium is important for the health of all species, humidity (air moisture level) requirements will vary from species to species depending on its habitat. Tropical rainforest species will require high humidity all year, while those from some subtropical or temperate areas will require variations in humidity depending on time of the year.

This is particularly important for species from those areas that experience pronounced wet and dry seasons. Species from arid and desert-like areas generally require low humidity throughout the year. The larger the water vessel in the terrarium, the greater the humidity will be, though heated and over-ventilated terraria tend to dry out very quickly. Desert-dwelling species should be provided with only a small dish of drinking water, as further humidity is not required. Conversely, rainforest and wet temperate forest species probably will require aids to maintaining high humidity. In addition to a large water vessel, you can spray regularly with a fine mist sprayer. An aquarium heater and an aerator in the water vessel will cause steady evaporation and its attendant high humidity. There are powered misting systems available for humidity-loving species. They tend to be expensive, but they can be helpful in keeping delicate chameleons, day geckos, and Monkey-tailed Skink healthy. In many situations it will be necessary to formulate a compromise situation between the ventilation and the humidity. Remember, however, that no lizards will thrive if they do not have access to dry surfaces.

This handsome lizard, *Agama minor,* is well suited for a naturalistic rocky terrarium. Photo by Aaron Norman.

FEEDING YOUR PETS

Lizards may be carnivorous, omnivorous, or mostly herbivorous, but the majority of species kept as pets fall into the first category. Most of the smaller lizards we keep will thrive on a variety of insects. Here the word variety is of utmost importance. As we know, all animals

Many lizards relish snails. The common garden snails, such as this *Helix aspersa*, are readily accepted "snacks." Photo by Ken Lucas

must have a balanced diet in order to keep in the best of health and to function properly. A balanced diet consists of macronutrients (proteins, fats, and carbohydrates) and so-called micronutrients (vitamins and minerals, many of which serve as catalysts to an animal's metabolism rather than true nutrients that are destroyed or modified during metabolism). Macronutrients form the bulk of a lizard's food, but the essential micronutrients are obtained through variety in the diet. You should ensure that you will have a continuing supply of the right types of food before you decide on what lizard species you wish to keep.

COLLECTING LIVE FOODS

While there are a number of excellent live food items that can be purchased from pet shops or propagated at home, it is recommended that wild-collected live foods be offered when available. Many collected insects are far more nutritious than home-bred ones, and the use of these as a dietary supplement will go a long way toward introducing the required variety into the diet.

If you live in a big city it may not be possible to collect live foods on a regular basis. Also, there usually is a shortage of wild live foods during the winter months in colder areas. However, country dwellers will be able to collect live foods on a regular basis, while city-dwellers will have to limit their collecting trips to the occasional day in the country. An hour or so spent collecting insects during a summer outing can be very productive. Some backyards and gardens can also often reveal a surprising amount of invertebrate life. You will find that not all lizards will take all food items, but it is worth experimenting.

One of the best ways of collecting a variety of insects and spiders is to use a sweep net. This is like a butterfly net, but preferably with a canvas reinforced rim as it is quite likely to get a fair amount of wear and tear. You can sweep the net through tall grass and the foliage of shrubs and trees. In productive areas you soon will collect a variety of caterpillars, moths, beetles, grasshoppers, spiders, and so on. These can be size-graded and placed in small glass or plastic jars for transport home. In hot weather it is advisable to place a little foliage in the jars in order to maintain moisture.

Another good method of collecting is to look under rocks, logs, and other ground litter. Here you will find a variety of spiders, crickets, pillbugs, earthworms, slugs, snails, and so on. These can be collected and transported as described above. If you don't like to touch the insects, you can use a spoon to scoop them directly into a jar. By breaking open rotten timber or tearing off the bark, you may find a number of insect grubs. In some areas you may be lucky enough to collect termites. The soft bodies of these "white ants" are a nutritious and readily accepted live food for many small insectivorous lizards.

Very small insects, for small or juvenile lizards, can be collected using a "pooter," which is a small plastic or glass jar with a suction tube fitted to it. This can be a cork with two holes, through each of which a plastic or metal tube passes. Two flexible rubber or plastic tubes are fitted over the tubes through the cork. The end of one of the flexible tubes is placed near the insects to be collected (often in the corolla of a flower where numerous small insects congregate), while the other is placed in the mouth. A sharp suck on the tube will cause the insects to be pulled into the jar. A piece of gauze placed over the mouth end will prevent you from getting an unwelcome meal!

Spiders are common in many areas and add variety to the diets of insect-eating lizards. This is a species of sac spider in the genus *Castianeria*. Photo by Paul Freed

RAISED LIVE FOODS

Over the past few years, the pet trade has shown an increasing interest in propagating several species of invertebrate foods especially for the welfare of captive insectivorous animals.

These are obtainable by quantity, weight, or volume, depending on the species. Some establishments sell by mail order, and others even sell cultures with instructions on how to further propagate them. You must decide for yourself whether you have the time and patience to cultivate your own live foods, or whether you want to buy small quantities on a regular basis. The following is a brief summary of some of the more commonly used live foods, with notes on their culture.

Crickets

These insects often are the main standby live food for insectivorous lizards. They are very nutritious and not difficult to breed. There are several species, but the best known is the common domestic cricket, *Acheta domesticus*. Adult crickets are about 2.5 cm (1 in) in length, while the hatchlings are about 3 mm (0.12 in), and there are several intermediate nymphal stages, giving a useful choice of sizes. Cricket cultures can be purchased quite easily. The insects are best kept in screened boxes or plastic bins furnished with old egg cartons or crumpled newspapers to act as hiding places. The crickets should be fed on a diet of cereal (bran, poultry meal, cornmeal, etc.) and a small amount of fresh vegetables daily (lettuce, carrot, apple, etc.). They will obtain most of their moisture from their food, but to be on the safe side it is advisable to provide them with a saucer or shallow dish containing a water-soaked sponge or cotton wadding (the insects will drown in open water)

Katydids are a nutritious food for lizards that are easy to find in the spring and summer. Small ones are common and giant ones can be found occasionally. Photo by M. Gilroy

Crickets form the bulk of many captive lizards' diets. Feed only as many crickets to your pet as it will eat at once; leftover crickets can get hungry enough to bite and injure a lizard.

so that they can drink if necessary. If maintained at a temperature around 26°C (79°F), the crickets will breed readily. The females may lay their eggs in a tray with moist sand or loose soil about 3 cm deep, and these normally hatch in about three weeks. It is best to remove the tray of eggs to a separate bin so that they are not eaten by the adults.

Mealworms

These have long been a standard live food for captive reptiles and birds. Relatively recent studies have shown that mealworms are not quite as nutritious as they might be due to an imbalance in their calcium to phosphorus ratio. However,

mealworms can still be considered an important part of a varied diet and can be nutritionally improved by adding a powdered vitamin/ mineral supplement to their growing medium. Mealworms are the larvae of a flour beetle, *Tenebrio molitor*. They can be kept in shallow, screened boxes, with a 5-cm (2-in) layer of bran/oatmeal or bran/cornmeal mixture. A bit of fresh greens or vegetables placed daily on the surface of the growing medium will supply the larvae with adequate moisture. Though relatively slow-growing, mealworms will breed readily. Allow some of the worms to grow to full size and pupate. After a few weeks they will emerge as adult mealworm beetles (which in themselves are also acceptable to

Giant or King Mealworms are available at many pet stores. They are not as easy to culture as their smaller kin. Photo by David J. Zoffer.

many lizards). The beetles soon will mate and lay eggs that will hatch into tiny mealworms. The whole process takes place in the growing medium and, under favorable conditions, you should get a new generation every two to three months. They are best kept at a temperature of around 26°C (79°F). Be careful that humidity in the container does not increase to the point where fungus begins to grow in the culture.

Locusts

These are large grasshoppers that are serious agricultural pests in many parts of the world and, as such, have been subject to much scientific study. This means that many laboratories breed them in large numbers for experimental purposes and they frequently are available on the "pet food" market, at least in Europe; presently they

Many larger lizards readily devour locusts. This is an African variety. Photo by Mark Smith

It is easy to collect caterpillars in many areas. Some varieties can be ordered through biological supply companies. Photo by Mark Smith.

are uncommon foods in the United States. Like crickets, they are a nutritious form of live food for captive insectivorous lizards and, as the adults are relatively large (7.5 cm, 3 in), they are suitable for larger lizards. Like crickets, the nymphal stages come in various sizes. Locusts are kept in heated cages (an old aquarium is ideal) at about 28°C (82°F) and fed on oatmeal and grass stems. The stems are placed in a jar of water to keep them fresh and should be changed daily; pack cotton wadding around the mouth of the jar to keep the insects from drowning. Trays of just barely moist sand about 7.5 cm (3 in) deep should be provided for egg-laying.

Fuzzy mice are newborn mice that have only recently grown their fur. Many larger lizards such as monitors and tegus are fed mice exclusively.

Silkworms

These have been bred intensively in the Orient for many generations and are the source of fine silk that is spun out of the cocoons made by the pupating larvae. Silkworms often are used in school biology classes and are fairly obtainable. The silkworms are the caterpillars of the silk moth, and both the larvae and the adult moths are useful as food for many lizards. The caterpillars feed on the foliage of mulberry trees. Leafy twigs from the tree can be placed in a jar of water to keep

Polymita venusta, an edible snail that can be fed to lizards. Blue-Tongued Skinks are avid snail-eaters.

A variety of mixed vegetables and fruits can be offered daily to herbivorous lizards. Photo by Isabelle Francais

them fresh and placed in a screened cage. Net material wrapped around a wire frame will confine your culture admirably. Replace the mulberry twigs as necessary.

Fruitflies

These are essential if you are raising small juvenile lizards. They also are accepted by some of the smaller species of adult lizards. In summer you usually can collect fruitflies by putting a box of banana skins or rotting fruit in a remote corner of the garden. As the flies accumulate you can whisk them up in a fine-meshed net. You also may be able to obtain a fruitfly culture, plus instructions and culture media, from a specialist supplier advertising in reptile magazines.

Vertebrate Foods

Mice, rats, chickens, pigeons, quail, and so on often are used as food for some of the larger lizards, especially monitors, large agamids, and some iguanas. Pinkie mice (juveniles that have not yet developed fur) are very useful food items for many smaller lizards. You can purchase supplies of vertebrate food items from many pet shops, where they are sold both living and frozen. Some companies specialize in killed, frozen mice, rats, and chicks. These should be thoroughly thawed out before being fed to your pets. In general it is better to feed such items to lizards rather than using strips of chicken or beef meat that do not

constitute a balanced diet. Pinkies and other vertebrate foods contain a large amount of calcium (from the skeleton).

VEGETABLE FOODS

Herbivorous and omnivorous lizards require a variety of vegetable foods. While green food such as lettuce may be taken eagerly by some lizards, this is not very nutritious and should be only a small part of a diet containing various fruits, vegetables, buds, and flowers. Give your lizards a mixture of chopped items and see what they prefer to eat. This will allow you to develop a feeding strategy.

Whatever the diet of your lizards, it should be regularly supplemented with a good vitamin/mineral preparation. Powdered preparations can be sprinkled over the food before you give it to the lizards. A supplement about twice per week should be adequate.

FREQUENCY OF FEEDING

It is difficult to lay down any hard and fast rules regarding how often you feed your lizards. In general it can be said that juvenile lizards and small species should be fed daily. This also applies to species that are largely herbivorous. Two or three sizable meals per week are usually adequate for large carnivorous lizards. Beware not to overfeed your lizards; this will lead to obesity and associated problems. It is better to err on the "too little" rather than on the "too much" side.

CARING FOR SICK LIZARDS

As long as your pet lizards are given optimum conditions in which to live and are provided with a suitable balanced diet, they are unlikely to get sick. Indeed, most cases of sickness are often directly or indirectly related to poor husbandry. In the past, when we knew much less about captive reptile welfare, many lizards were lost within a few weeks of their acquisition because of ignorance on the part of the keeper.

PREVENTION IS BETTER THAN CURE

It is much better to know the causes of ill health and to prevent sickness rather than having to worry about curing an outbreak of disease when it happens. The provision of correct environmental conditions and provision of a proper diet will go a long way toward keeping our lizards healthy. Lizards kept in unsuitable conditions will suffer stress, their natural immunities will diminish, and they will be open to infection.

General Hygiene

It should go without saying that cages must be kept as clean as possible. Feces must be removed daily and fresh water should always be available. Cages and furnishings should be stripped down and cleaned at regular intervals. This will include scrubbing the interior of the cage

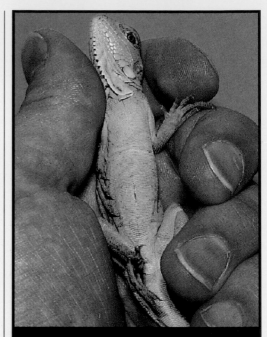

The proper way to hold small lizards. With the lizard held firmly, its health can be assessed and proper care administered. Photo by W. P. Mara

and the furnishings with a weak solution of household bleach and thoroughly rinsing off with warm water and drying out before the lizards are replaced. Try and keep the furnishing arrangements fairly constant; lizards tend to get to know well what they regard as their territory and will be confused if you make changes every time you clean out the cage. Personal hygiene is also important. Keep an old set of clothes to wear when servicing your terraria. Always wash your hands before moving from one terrarium to the next.

Handling

Most lizards prefer not to be handled, though there are a few species that don't seem to mind too much. Most of the more commonly kept pet lizards will become accustomed to being handled on a regular basis as long as you are quiet and gentle in your actions. In the case of small, delicate, or nervous lizards such as anoles and geckos it is best not to handle them at all unless strictly necessary. It is much better to admire them by sight only, rather than to risk stressing them by too much handling. Lizards that are handled too much are much less likely to breed than those that are left undisturbed.

Small lizards up to about 15 cm (6 in) in length can be cupped in the hands and examined by opening the fingers. Some of the more lively little characters can be difficult to restrain without injuring them, so you may require some practice. Most lizards will attempt to bite if they are unused to handling, but those in the small range are incapable of giving more than a little nip that is unlikely to break the skin.

Medium sized lizards, from 15 cm (6 in) to about 45 cm (18 in), should be grasped around the thorax gently but firmly while restraining the head with the thumb and forefinger to prevent biting. Some lizards in this group are capable of giving a fairly powerful and painful bite, and sometimes the skin will be broken. Accidental bites should be swabbed with an antiseptic solution and covered with small bandages to them clean.

The range of good nutritional and health care products available to keepers of reptiles and amphibians continues to grow as professionals in the field expand their knowledge of herps' needs. Photo: Courtesy of Mardel Laboratories, Inc.

Water bowls must be kept clean to prevent disease. A solution of bleach and soapy water will safely disinfect them. Rinse well. Photo by Isabelle Francais

Acquiring Pet Lizards

Most pet lizards today are purchased from pet shops, specialist dealers, or breeders. The days of collecting specimens from the wild are almost over, as most of the popular pet species are protected in Northern Hemisphere countries, and personal importation of "pets" collected or bought during that vacation to the tropics has become more complicated. One time you will need to handle lizards is when you give them their pre-purchase inspection. This will be necessary because you want to be sure that the lizards are healthy from the outset. Examine your prospective purchases carefully. Do not buy from dealers with dirty or overcrowded cages. Do not buy emaciated lizards even if you think you can save them. Tell-tale signs of sick or malnourished lizards are sunken eyes, lethargy, hollow abdomens, dull, loose skin, and hollows at the tail base. Make sure the eyes are bright and clear; that the mouth and the vent are clean and uninfected; and that the skin is unbroken and unblemished. Inspect the joints and digits for signs of articular gout (lameness and/or hard lumps in the joints) and ensure that the animal is alert and lively.

Taking Them Home

Once you have purchased your stock, you must try and get it home and into its new quarters as soon as possible. Lizards usually are transported in soft cloth bags that are tied at the top with a

However, a practiced lizard keeper should be able to easily handle his lizards without getting bitten.

Large lizards from about 45 cm (18 in) to 1 m (40 in) or more are not recommended for beginners. Most large iguanas and monitors, unless they are hand-tame, will bite and scratch fiercely if given the chance. They should be grasped firmly around the neck with one hand and lifted bodily with the other hand. The tail and hindlimbs can be restrained by tucking them under the elbow. Bites and scratches from large lizards can cause severe lacerations that may require medical attention, so be careful!

Children must be taught to wash their hands after handling reptiles to prevent a *Salmonella* infection. Supervision is essential. Photo by Isabelle Francais

knot or tape. Each lizard preferably should be placed in its own bag and the bags placed in a cardboard box. Don't leave your lizards in situations where they will get too cold or too hot; many a lizard in its bag has been lost by leaving it in a cold car overnight or in hot sun during the day.

QUARANTINE

If you have just acquired your first lizards you can place them directly into their newly prepared home. However, if you already have lizards and you have acquired additional specimens, it is important to keep them in isolation for a period of three weeks or more before introducing them to any of your existing stock. This period of quarantine is to ensure that your new lizards are not sickening from any infectious disease that could

infect all of your stock. Even though you may have been very vigilent in your initial health inspection, there is a small chance that you may have missed something or that an animal is infected in its early stages and not yet showing any symptoms. A quarantine cage should be placed in a room separate from your main collection. It should be simply furnished but have all of the necessary life-support systems. If quarantined lizards show no signs of disease after three weeks, it usually is safe to house them in their more permanent quarters.

DISEASES AND TREATMENTS

Although we will have tried our utmost to prevent outbreaks of

Even this feisty Tokay Gecko should be quarantined before introduction into an established collection. Photo by Karl H. Switak

disease, unfortunate incidents may happen from time to time. Many veterinarians recently have been turning their attentions to some of the more exotic kinds of pets, and there are those who specialize in reptiles. Though your local veterinarian may not be an expert on lizards, he will most likely be able to communicate with one who is knowledgeable. Lizards are valuable and deserve the best of treatment. Whenever in doubt about the health of your pets, please be sure to obtain the appropriate veterinary advice rather than take do-it-yourself measures. The following is a brief summary of the more common diseases and conditions of captive lizards.

Towels are useful for restraining defensive lizards during any necessary handling. This is *Corucia zebrata*, the Prehensile-tailed Skink Photo by Karl H. Switak.

The neck of this Green Iguana, *Iguana iguana,* has been badly burned, probably from contact with a heat lamp. Photo by Anthony L. Del Prete

Wounds and Injuries

Wounds and broken bones may be caused by fighting, by attempting to escape, by being crushed by falling objects in the cage, or by burning. Most injuries are preventable. Some wounds may need to be swabbed with a mild veterinary antiseptic such as povidone iodine. Deeper wounds and broken bones will require treatment and possibly surgery by your veterinarian.

Nutritional Diseases

These occur as a result of an inadequate diet and should not happen if you feed your animals properly. Most of the conditions arise as the result of a deficiency in various vitamins or minerals due to insufficient variety in the diet, while some occur as a result of an overabundance of animal protein or calcium. With a variety of the correct types of food, additional vitamins and minerals, fresh water, and the opportunity to bask in sunlight or artificial sunlight, you should not have problems with such conditions.

Abscesses

Soft lumps developing below the skin are abscesses caused by infections entering through a small wound. Untreated, some abscesses can literally eat away the flesh. Abscesses often require veterinary antibiotic treatment and/or surgery.

A pair of ticks. The large one is fully engorged with the host's blood. Photo by Ken Lucas

Ticks and Mites

These arachnid pests are the most common external parasites of lizards. Wild-caught specimens often have ticks attached to them. They should be removed by first dabbing with a little alcohol to loosen their mouthparts, then gently pulling them out of the skin.

Mites can be the bane of the lizard keeper. These tiny, globular parasites are smaller than a pinhead and can proliferate to large numbers in the terrarium before they are even noticed. Numerous mites can cause stress, anemia, dermatitis, and shedding problems. Additionally, the mites can transmit pathogenic organisms from the blood of one lizard to the next. Once a mite infestation has been ascertained, the animals should be treated

A colony of mites living behind the ear of a Crevice Spiny Lizard, *Sceloporus poinsetti*. Photo by Paul Freed

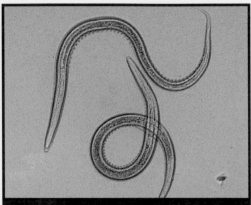

Hookworm larvae found in a *Boa constrictor*. Photo by E. Rundquist

of your lizards checked for worms in a veterinary laboratory. Infestations can be treated with proprietory vermicides available from your veterinarian.

Enteric Infections

Various enteric diseases are caused by a host of bacteria and

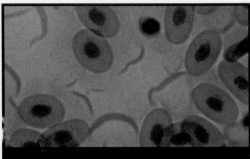

Parasites in the blood of a Timber Rattlesnake, *Crotalus horridus*. Photo by Paul Freed

with a suitable chemical available from your pet shop. Terraria should be stripped down and thoroughly disinfected.

Worm Infections

Most wild lizards play host to one or more species of intestinal worms. Under normal conditions the relationship is symbiotic and little harm is done to the host. Under stress, however, worm infestations of the intestine can be dangerous, resulting in compaction, malnutrition, and anemia. To be on the safe side it is advisable to have fecal samples

protozoa. These include salmonellosis (food poisoning), which can be transmitted to humans (all the more reason for sound personal hygiene). Lizards suffering from enteric infections will show signs of lethargy and general debilitation coupled with diarrhea. Such infections require immediate veterinary attention.

An amoebic cyst found in a Water Monitor, *Varanus salvator*. Photo by E. Rundquist

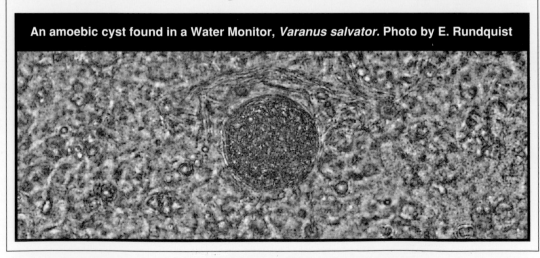

LIZARD PROPAGATION

Due to the increasing reduction in numbers of many lizard species in the wild, it is essential that captive breeding programs should be developed and maintained. Unfortunate as it may seem, it appears that some species may only survive under the protection of captive environments unless more serious conservation measures are taken now. Many lizard species now are regularly bred in captivity, but, in contrast to other kinds of domestic animals, there is still much to be learned about lizard propagation. What we do know is that lizards are unlikely to breed unless they are provided with the kinds of environmental and seasonal conditions prevailing in their native habitats.

Many lizards from temperate and subtropical areas rely on a period of winter hibernation to bring them into breeding condition. It is not necessary for such lizards to complete a full period of hibernation in captivity, and a short "rest period" at cooler temperatures will provide a satisfactory compromise. This can be accomplished by gradually decreasing the temperature and photoperiod in the terrarium over several days while reducing feeding. You should aim to get the temperature down to about 10°C (50°F) for most temperate species or 15°C (59°F) for many subtropical species. It will help if you know something about the climates of your lizards' native habitats. You can get such information from a good geographical atlas. During the cooling period, the lizards will become lethargic and will hide away in their shelters. When you wish to end the compromise hibernation period, which can be anything from two to three months long, you should reverse the procedures described above, gradually bringing the temperature back to optimum over a period of several days and also increasing the photoperiod. As soon as the lizards become active you can begin to feed them again.

COURTSHIP AND MATING

As most lizards live fairly solitary lives for most of the year, it is often best to keep the sexes separate until you wish them to breed. The sudden introduction of a female to a male in his own territory often will initiate a breeding response. In some cases the introduction of two females to two males will further increase the possibilities of mating as the territorial instincts of the males against each other will fool them into mating "before the opponent gets a chance."

Courtship procedures among lizards vary from species to species. A standard courtship sequence is that a sexually

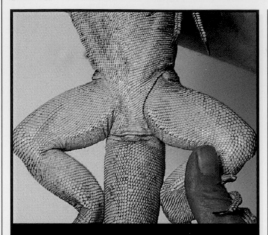

The enlarged pores on the thighs (femoral pores) of this Green Iguana, *Iguana iguana,* indicate that it is a male. Photo by Isabelle Francais.

MALE OR FEMALE?

One very important parameter to breeding success is the possession of a true pair, at least one male and one female. While a very few species have been shown to be able to reproduce without male fertilization (parthenogenetic), the vast majority practice sexual reproduction. Many lizard species show some differences between the sexes. These may include variations in general size, color, shape, tail length, behavior, and so on. In some species the presence or absence of femoral or pre-anal pores will give a clue. As the male hemipenes are inverted into the base of the tail when dormant, this usually means a male has a correspondingly thicker tail base than the female. In some cases the presence of hemipenes can be detected by

Everting the hemipenes of a male blue-tongued skink, *Tiliqua* sp. Have an experienced person show you how to do this, as it is possible to injure the animal. Photo by Isabelle Francais.

aroused male will approach his intended mate and display to her. This may include head bobbing, tail waggling, and bodily contortions all meant to impress the female, which more often than not will appear to ignore his attentions or even run away. After a while the male attempts to grasp the female in his jaws, usually on the neck or upper back. Once subdued, the female will allow him to bend the rear part of his body beneath hers so that their corresponding cloacal regions come into apposition, enabling him to insert one of his erect hemipenes into her cloaca.

Depending on the species, copulation may take anything from a few minutes to several hours. In some cases lizard mating appears rather a violent affair, but this is quite natural and serious injuries rarely occur. Never try to intervene in the procedure or the mating may not be successful.

Hatching Rough-Scaled Geckos, *Pachydactylus rugosus*. Photo by Paul Freed

Others lay them under rocks, logs, or other ground litter, while most geckos lay their small, hard-shelled eggs in crevices in tree bark.

You must supply your captive lizards with suitable facilities for egg-laying. In the case of geckos, a few pieces of rough tree bark will offer a choice. Other species should be offered a deep container of moist sand in which they may excavate a laying burrow. Some individuals may not be happy with what you have offered and will end up scattering their eggs all over the substrate in apparent frustration. You should keep careful watch at egg-laying time so that you can remove the eggs for artificial incubation. With the exception of the eggs of geckos, eggs left to incubate in the terrarium are rarely successful.

With the exception of the geckos, which lay hard-shelled

squeezing gently at the tail base, causing them to partially evert. Of course, in many lizards squeezing the tail immediately results in autotomy, so perhaps this is not such a wise move after all.

CARE OF EGGS

Once successfully fertilized, eggs will begin to develop in the female. She will become progressively plumper as the eggs increase in size, and eventually you may be able to see and feel the eggs pressing against the sides of her abdomen. The speed at which the eggs develop will depend on species and conditions and may vary from 30 to more than 100 days. Wild lizards seek out suitable spots in which to lay their eggs. Areas that can supply the necessary concealment, warmth, and humidity seem to be the main requirements. Most lizards excavate burrows in soft soil in which to lay their eggs.

Hatching Desert Spiny Lizards, *Sceloporus magister*. Photo by Ken Lucas.

eggs, most lizard species lay soft, leathery-shelled eggs. These are designed to absorb moisture from the substrate or incubation medium and actually will fill out, increasing in size and weight as incubation progresses.

I have found vermiculite, an inert, absorbent, granular insulation material, to be by far the best incubation material, but success with sand, peat, or sphagnum moss also is possible. Vermiculite can be mixed with its own weight of water and placed in a plastic incubation box with just a few ventilation holes punched in the lid (it is important to have some air movement without losing too much humidity). The eggs are partially buried in the vermiculite, with about one-third of their surface area exposed to allow regular inspection.

The egg box should be placed in a heated incubator, the interior of which is maintained at 25-30°C (77-86°F). Several makes of suitable incubators are available on the market, but I have successfully used a lidded Styrofoam fruit box partially filled with water. Two bricks are placed in the water so that they break the water surface, and the egg box is placed on top of these. The water is heated with a thermostatically controlled

A juvenile *Riopa fernandi*, an African skink that lives in tropical forests. Photo by R. D. Bartlett

Like many other neonatal lizards, this White-Throated Monitor, *Varanus albigularis "ionides,"* will get considerably duller as it grows. Photo by R. D. Bartlett.

aquarium heater. Adjust the heater until the air in the chamber can be maintained at the required temperature. You will require a good thermometer in order to do this. A glass tank or a wooden box could also be used as an incubator, and you have a choice of all kinds of heaters, from lamps to cables, pads to panels. Whatever you use, you must maintain the optimum temperature thermostatically and ensure that humidity remains high around the eggs.

Eggs may take from 30 to 100 days to hatch, again depending on species and conditions. You must inspect the eggs regularly, but do not move them about unnecessarily. You must be especially vigilant as hatching time approaches so that you can remove the babies to nursery housing when they hatch.

LIVEBEARING LIZARDS

Some species give birth to fully formed juveniles rather than lay eggs. Such species are described as ovoviviparous, which means that the embryos develop full term in the mother's body and hatch from their membranous eggs just before, during, or just after deposition. This makes life somewhat easier for the breeder of such lizards as the period of

Here are an adult and a hatchling Fat-tailed Gecko, *Hemitheconyx caudinctus*. Keep baby lizards separate from adults who may eat them. Photo by Paul Freed.

artificial incubation is dispensed with. However, as some adult livebearers have no qualms about adding their own youngsters to the menu, it is best to remove them to separate accommodations as soon as possible after birth.

REARING THE YOUNG

Whether hatched from eggs or live-born, juvenile lizards are best raised separately from the adults in their own cages. Tiny lizards can be housed in small plastic boxes that are stored in a larger heated chamber. Screening is glued over holes in the lids of the plastic boxes to allow for adequate ventilation, plus the admittance of broad-spectrum lighting for those species that require it. You will require a variety of very small insects, such as hatchling crickets or fruitflies, for the tiniest of these reptiles. During the initial period of growth a balanced diet is extremely important. You should shake powdered vitamin/mineral supplement over the food insects about twice per week. Provide the youngsters with a very shallow dish of water that must be changed regularly.

Hatchling Water Dragons, *Physignathus cocincinus*, basking. The dark one is a melanistic individual. Photo by Paul Freed.

SOME SUGGESTED SPECIES

With about 20 families, 350 genera, and over 3000 species, lizards form the largest group of reptiles. In this small introductory work it is possible to include only a token number of all species. The species I have selected to discuss here are those that frequently are available; most also are extensively bred in captivity. I also have included a few of my favorites that may be available occasionally. The lengths given are the maximum head and tail lengths one would expect to find; in many cases the average length is somewhat shorter.

FAMILY GEKKONIDAE—THE GECKOS

With about 800 species and subspecies, this is one of the largest lizard families. Geckos have colonized most parts of the tropics and parts of some temperate regions. Some typical characteristics of geckos are their adhesive toe pads that allow them to run over smooth vertical surfaces and even to move upside-down on ceilings, etc. Most geckos lack movable eyelids and have a transparent spectacle like snakes. Most species are nocturnal. Many geckos make ideal pets for the home terrarium

Impressive coloration and a voracious appetite explain the popularity of the Tokay Gecko, *Gekko gecko.* Photo by Karl H. Switak.

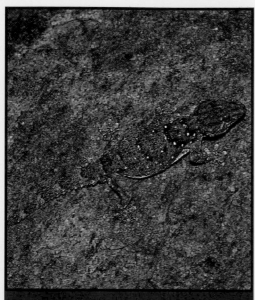

Bibron's Gecko, *Pachydactylus bibroni,* is a very hardy lizard that occasionally has been bred in captivity. Photo by Karl H. Switak

and some frequently are bred in captivity.

Tokay Gecko
Gekko gecko
Length: 35 cm (14 in). One of the largest gecko species, the Tokay is frequently available and is regularly bred in captivity. Being a member of the subfamily Gekkoninae (as are the next three species described), it has the typical main gecko features. Hailing from the jungles of Southeast Asia, this spectacular species has a robust head and body and a relatively slender tail. The color is slaty blue, covered rather evenly with large pink to orange spots. Though they are generally hardy in captivity, Tokay

Frequently available and inexpensive, African House Geckos, *Hemidactylus mabouia,* make great pets for beginners. Photo by R. D. Bartlett.

Geckos have an aggressive and unfriendly disposition and will not hesitate to bite. They are therefore to be admired rather than petted. They are named after their loud "to-keh" call that usually occurs at night. A pair of Tokays should be kept in a tall, semihumid terrarium with dimensions at least 50 x 50 x 90 (20 x 20 x 36 in). Provide several climbing branches. Maintain the temperature at 25-30°C (77-86°F) during the day, reduced to around 20°C (68°F) at night. Tokays are voracious feeders and will take a variety of invertebrates. Large specimens may take pinkie mice.

The beautiful Boehme's Giant Day Gecko, *Phelsuma madagascariensis boehmi,* requires broad-spectrum lighting to stay in good health. Photo by R. D. Bartlett.

Phelsuma lineata, the Lined Day Gecko, is a handsome small day gecko that is occasionally available. The care of this species is similar to that of the Giant Day Gecko. Since it is smaller, it needs smaller insects and can be kept in a smaller terrarium. Photo by A. Norman.

Bibron's Gecko
Pachydactylus bibroni

Length: 18 cm (7 in). This species is extremely hardy in captivity and is available from time to time. A native of southern Africa, it is mainly crepuscular but frequently is active during the day as well as at dusk and dawn. It is an inhabitant of semiarid woodlands where it lives largely on the trunks and branches of trees or among rocks, concealing itself in hollows and beneath bark. It has a compact body, well-developed toe pads, and a relatively short, thick tail. Color varies through various shades of brown, with a sprinkling of raised light and dark scales. It requires a small cage with adequate hiding places (rocks, branches) and a small water dish. It may be fed on a variety of insects and spiders with a regular vitamin/mineral supplement.

House Gecko
Hemidactylus mabouia

Length 20 cm (8 in). Originating in southern Africa, this species has successfully colonized many parts of Central America and eastern South America. It is one of several species in its genus that often are available. In the wild it frequently is found in and around human habitations, where it often is encouraged due to its insectivorous habits. It is a fairly slender gecko with a soft, delicate, almost transparent skin that is scattered with enlarged granular scales. It is gray to gray-brown with faint darker markings. Most Hemidactylus species are hardy terrarium inmates and will live for several years if given the right conditions. Temperature should be maintained around 28°C (82°F) during the day and reduced to 23°C (74°F) at night. A fairly humid atmosphere is essential, so supply a large water bowl and/or mist spray regularly. All species in the genus will feed on a variety of small invertebrates.

Madagascar Giant Day Gecko
Phelsuma madagascariensis

Length: 25 cm (10 in). Probably the largest and most often available of the several species of day gecko, this species occurs on the island of Madagascar, where it is becoming scarcer due to forest clearance. The ground color is leaf-green, which may be uniform or patterned with red or white patches, making them very attractive lizards. They are active during the day and have round pupils, as opposed to the vertical pupils of nocturnal species. They require a tall, humid, planted terrarium with temperatures in the range 25-30°C (77-86°F), reduced a little at night. They may be fed on a variety of insects and nectar. A good supplement to give them is a 50/50 solution of honey in water provided in a small shallow dish; a sugar lump to which a drop of liquid vitamin/ mineral supplement has been added also may be licked. As these geckos have high calcium requirements they should be given a separate small dish of crushed cuttlebone so that they can help themselves when the need arises.

Leopard Gecko
Eublepharis macularius

Length: 25 cm (10 in). This is a large, robust species beautifully patterned with black spots and blotches on a brown or yellow background. Juveniles have a totally different pattern of dark and light bands. It is a member of a subfamily of geckos (Eublepharinae) that are atypical in having eyelids and lacking adhesive toe pads. A regular terrarium subject that is captive-bred on a regular basis, this species is easy to obtain. Native to the arid steppes of Afghanistan, Pakistan, and northwestern India, it requires a fairly dry terrarium but should be supplied with a small dish of drinking water. It will do well with daytime temperatures up to 30°C (86°F), reduced to 20°C (68°F) at night. It will feed on a variety of invertebrates and is especially fond of crickets. A simulated hibernation period at reduced temperatures for a few weeks in the winter will induce breeding.

Leopard Geckos, *Eublepharis macularius,* have endearing faces and can be very docile. Photo by Karl W. Switak

FAMILY IGUANIDAE—THE IGUANAS

At one time containing about 60 genera and over 700 species, it seems that the Iguanidae has now been reduced to just eight genera, while the remaining genera have been allocated to several other families. Most members of the "new" Iguanidae are relatively large, robust lizards with spiny crests. They are native to the mainland of North, Central, and South America, the West indies, the Galapagos Islands, and the islands of Fiji and Tonga.

Green Iguana
Iguana iguana

Length: 160 cm (63 in). These must be among the best known and most revered of pet lizards due to their bizarre and attractive appearance, good temperament, and relative ease of keeping. Native to Central America and northern South America, they have threatened status in many areas due to deforestation and collection for the food and pet

This Leopard Gecko has an aberrant yellow coloration. Breeders often select for odd colors and patterns in this species. Photo by R. D. Bartlett, courtesy of B. Brant

The dinosaur of the living room: the Green Iguana, *Iguana iguana.* Photo by Anthony L. Del Prete

trades. Recent attempts at protecting the species in the wild in some areas should help alleviate the problem. The Green Iguana is a robust lizard with a spiny crest extending from the back of the head along the spine and onto the tail. The male possesses a large, leathery dewlap that it can erect during aggression or sexual activity. Adults are a basic gray-green in color with darker bands, sometimes with bluish or rust highlights. Juveniles are a stunning leaf-green up to about a year of age before they begin to develop the more somber adult coloration. A pair of adult Green Iguanas requires a terrarium with a minimum size of 180 cm long x 180 cm high x 90 cm deep

This handsome baby Green Iguana will need a varied diet and broad-spectrum lighting if it is to thrive. Photo by Marian Bacon.

(approx 6 ft x 6 ft x 3 ft). It should be furnished with a large water vessel and strong branches for climbing. Daytime temperatures should be maintained at 25-30°C (77-86°F), reduced a little at night but never less than 18°C (65°F). Juvenile iguanas are partially insectivorous, but become increasingly more herbivorous as they grow. Adults can be fed on a variety of green foods (fruits and vegetables) cut into bite-sized pieces. Tame specimens will try almost everything from steak and kidney pie to peaches and cream, but such items are best kept to a minimum if you don't want your pets to become overweight. Current research indicates that adult Green Iguanas need no animal protein in the diet and young specimens also can do well without it.

Like its relative the Green Iguana, the Chuckwalla, *Sauromalus obesus*, is mostly herbivorous. Photo by Karl H. Switak

Chuckwalla
Sauromalus obesus

Length: 45 cm (18 in). This desert-dwelling iguanid occurs in the southwestern USA and Mexico, where it lives among rocky outcrops. It is a rather portly lizard that likes to hide in rock crevices when disturbed, taking in air and jamming itself into the cavity, making it extremely difficult to remove. The basic color of the Chuckwalla varies depending on its range; it may be uniformly blackish brown to reddish orange with a dark head and shoulders, sometimes with a black banded, white tail. It requires a dry desert terrarium with basking areas to 40°C (104°F) during the day, but reduced dramatically at night to around 20°C (68°F). Provide a small dish of drinking water and some flat rocks arranged to form crevices. Chuckwallas are almost exclusively vegetarian and should be provided with a range of green foods, including dandelion flowers, fruit, and cactus pads if available.

Desert Iguana
Dipsosaurus dorsalis

Length: 40 cm (16 in). This is another desert-dwelling species from the southwestern USA and northern Mexico. It lives in arid scrubland. Though not so portly looking as the Chuckwalla, it is nevertheless a robust lizard. It is a light buff in color with irregular white spots and bars. When basking in full sun it becomes

Desert Iguanas, *Dipsosaurus dorsalis,* require very high temperatures and broad-spectrum lighting. Photo by Ken Lucas

very light colored, appearing almost white. Its terrarium requirements are as described for the Chuckwalla, and hot day basking temperatures are essential. As well as a general vegetarian diet, I have found them to be partial to the young shoots of pungent herbs such as sage and rosemary. Some also will take insects.

Green or Plumed Basilisk
Basiliscus plumifrons
Length: 65 cm (26 in). The four or five species of basilisks have been removed from the Iguanidae to a new family (Corytophanidae). The Plumed

Basilisk must be one of the most bizarre looking of all lizards and, as such, is a prize terrarium exhibit. Native to the steamy rain forests of southern Central America, it is a tree-dweller but will not hesitate to take to water if danger threatens, often running so fast on its hind legs over the water surface that it does not sink for several meters. It also can swim very well if the occasion arises. It is a streamlined lizard with long limbs and has a double crest on its head, a high crest along its back, and another along the tail (muuch lower in females than males). The ground color is bright green with bluish spots and highlights (much more subdued in females), with a bright golden yellow eye. Basilisks require a humid, tropical rainforest terrarium with a large water vessel and adequate climbing facilities. Daytime temperatures can rise as high as 30°C (86°F), but reduce to about 24°C (75°F) at night. They feed on a variety of invertebrates; large specimens will take pinkie mice or even small, live freshwater fish.

Helmeted Iguana
Corytophanes cristatus

Length: 35 cm (14 in). Members of this genus have been placed in the newly formed family Corytophanidae along with the basilisks and casque-headed iguanas (*Laemanctus*). *C. cristatus* occurs in the southern parts of Central America, living in the tree canopy, but with less reliance on water than the basilisks. The slender body is laterally compressed. The "helmet" extends as a spiny ridge from the top of each eye and joins at the neck, where the spines continue down the back. The ground color is brown, marked with darker blotches and bands. These lizards should be housed in a humid rainforest terrarium, though only a small, shallow water vessel is required. The temperatures are as described for *Basiliscus*. Feed on a variety of invertebrates.

In appearance, Helmeted Iguanas, *Corytophanes cristatus*, recall the dragons of fantastic stories. Photo by Karl H. Switak

Green Basilisks, *Basiliscus plumifrons,* are beautiful but often high-strung lizards. A large enclosure is necessary. Photo by John C. Murphy

FAMILY AGAMIDAE—THE AGAMIDS

The agamids form the Old World versions of the iguanas, and many species show superficial resemblances to species of iguanas, having crests, dewlaps, and other interesting appendages. The family contains about 35 genera and over 300 species.

Asian Water Dragon
Physignathus cocincinus

Length: 75 cm (30 in). This popular species is being increasingly bred in captivity and should not be too difficult to obtain. Although not closely related, it bears a remarkable resemblance in shape and color to the Green Iguana. Native to Southeast Asia, the Water Dragon lives in wooded areas, usually close to permanent water. The basic color is green, often suffused with pink and blue tones around the throat and flanks. The long, tapering tail is banded with brown. It requires a large terrarium with a voluminous water vessel and stout climbing branches. It likes a daytime temperature up to 30°C (86°F), but this should be reduced at night to around 23°C (74°F). Unlike the Green Iguana, this

Water Dragons, *Physignathus cocincinus,* resemble Green Iguanas but are not closely related to them. Photo by Aaron Norman.

Inland Bearded Dragons, *Pogona vitticeps,* will readily breed if given a short winter cooling. Photo by R. D. Bartlett

species is almost totally carnivorous and should be fed on a variety of larger invertebrates as well as small mice. Some may take a small amount of soft, ripe fruit.

Bearded Dragon
Pogona barbata

Length 45 cm (18 in). Formerly known as *Amphibolurus barbatus*, this species is presently being captive-bred in small numbers. A native of eastern and southeastern Australia, its name arises from the large gular pouch or "beard" that it inflates when alarmed or territorially threatened. It is basically mottled gray and brown in color, paler when the lizard is basking. In the wild it occurs in a variety of habitats from woodland to open scrubland, often in arid areas. It requires a large terrarium with basking temperatures to 40°C (104°F), but should have cooler areas to retire to when necessary; reduce the temperature to room level at night. Broad-spectrum lighting should be provided. The Bearded Dragon will feed on a variety of invertebrates, pinkie mice, and sometimes a little ripe fruit. Provide it with a small dish of water. Over the past few years this species has been largely replaced in captivity by the Interior Bearded Dragon, *Pogona vitticeps,* a somewhat smaller species with a paler throat; it has been bred in very large numbers of late.

Spiny-tailed Agama
Uromastyx acanthinurus

Length: 35 cm (14 in). The bizarre appearance of this species makes it a prized terrarium subject, though it is not as readily available as it was in the past. It has a thick-set, flattened body, a broad head, and a short, thick, spiny tail. When at rest, its body color is dull olive-brown, but when basking it takes on a marbling of yellow and black, with the head almost jet-black. Native to North Africa, it often takes refuge in burrows. It requires a desert terrarium with a deep sandy substrate. Maintain the air temperature at 25-30°C (77-86°F) during day with the basking area to 40°C (104°F). Broad-spectrum lighting is essential. A small dish of water should be available. Almost totally herbivorous, it should be fed on a variety of fruits and vegetables; it may take the occasional mealworm or cricket. Difficult feeders can often be tempted with yellow flowers, especilly dandelions.

Some African Spiny-Tailed Agamas, *Uromastyx acanthinurus,* will eat softened bird seed as a supplement to a varied vegetarian diet. Photo by Isabelle Francais

Leaf litter and soil is a good substrate for a terrarium with a Broad-Headed Skink, *Eumeces laticeps*. Photo by R. D. Bartlett.

FAMILY SCINCIDAE—THE SKINKS

This large family of lizards contains about 50 genera and over 600 species, with representatives on all continents except Antarctica. Most skinks are elongate, circular in cross-section, and have a long tapering tail and short limbs. However, exceptions include species with relatively short tails or with reduced or absent limbs.

Broad-headed Skink
Eumeces laticeps

Length 30 cm (12 in). This, one of the largest US skinks, occurs in the southeastern quarter of the country. It has a robust body and, as its name implies, a broad head. The body color is brown, with five stripes that become fainter with age. The male has a red head. In juveniles, the tail is bright blue, changing to brown with maturity. They live in open woodlands and are partially arboreal, foraging for insects among the foliage of trees and taking refuge beneath bark or in tree hollows. They require a medium sized woodland terrarium with temperatures in the range 21-24°C (70-75°F) plus additional basking facilities. Reduce the temperature at night. Provide a shallow water vessel and feed on a range of invertebrates and pinkie mice.

As the name implies, the Prehensile-tailed Skink, *Corucia zebrata,* has a strong, flexible tail that aids in climbing. Photo by Ken Lucas.

Prehensile-tailed Skink
Corucia zebrata

Length: 60 cm (24 in). This extraordinary skink is now becoming more readily available as the forests of the Solomon Islands come down at an alarming rate. As such it is a by-product of the devastating denudation of the land. If the species is to be saved it will probably be as a result of captive breeding, with which some success has already been achieved. The skink is arboreal and herbivorous, with a strong, prehensile tail. The basic color is olive to brown marked with darker stripes and blotches. It requires a tall, humid rainforest terrarium with facilities to climb. Daytime temperatures can be as high as 30°C (86°F), reduced to about 24°C (75°F) at night. Only a small drinking vessel is necessary. Feed on a variety of greenfood, including fruit and vegetables; it is especially fond of the leaves of large climbing pothos plants. A regular vitamin/mineral supplement is essential.

Eastern Blue-tongued Skink
Tiliqua scincoides

Length: 45 cm (18 in). This attractive, popular, and docile native of Australia is bred fairly regularly and is frequently available, though it may be expensive. It has a rather long, thick body, short limbs, and a broad head. The body color varies from brown to gray with light and dark transverse bars. It requires a large terrarium with a leaf litter or bark substrate and a water vessel in which it may bathe. Provide a

The Prehensile-tailed Skink is also sold under the names Solomon Island Skink and Monkey-Tailed Skink. Photo by Ken Lucas.

The Common Blue-tongued Skink, *Tiliqua scincoides,* makes a hardy and docile pet. Photo by Karl H. Switak

hiding cave or hollow log and a basking area to 35°C (95°F). Reduce the temperature to around 20°C (68°F) at night. Fairly easy to feed, the Eastern Blue-tongue will take a variety of invertebrates and is especially fond of snails and clean earthworms. It also will take soft fruit such as banana, minced lean beef, and canned cat or dog food.

FAMILY CORDYLIDAE—GIRDLED LIZARDS

So called because of the girdled or belted appearance of the large scales that are reinforced by bony scutes beneath, the family includes two subfamilies: Cordylinae, the typical girdled lizards, and Gerrhosaurinae, the

The Common Girdled Lizard, *C. cordylus,* can be kept in the same conditions as Jones's Armadillo Lizard, *C. jonesi.* Photo by R. D. Bartlett

plated lizards. All are native to Africa and Madagascar.

Jones' Armadillo Lizard
Cordylus jonesi

Length: 15 cm (6 in). Though one of the smaller members of the family, this native of southern Africa is one of the easiest captives. The body and limbs are furnished with large, spiny scales, with similar rings of scales along the tail. The head is triangular, with spines along the back edge. The color is plain brown on the back, whitish beneath. Breeding males may show a reddish tinge on the neck. It requires a

The Sungazer, *Cordylus giganteus,* is impressive but rarely offered for sale. Photo by Karl H. Switak

semidesert terrarium furnished with rocks and caves. Provide basking temperatures to 35°C (95°F), but ensure there are cooler spots. Reduce the temperature to around 20°C (68°F) at night. Feed on a range of small invertebrates and provide a small water vessel.

Yellow-throated Plated Lizard
Gerrhosaurus flavigularis

Length: 60 cm (24 in). Also native to southern Africa, this species lacks the spines of the

The Giant Plated Lizard, *Gerrhosaurus validus,* consumes a fair amount of vegetation as well as invertebrates. Photo by Karl H. Switak

armadillo lizards, the scales being arranged as squarish plates. If it can be obtained, this species makes an entertaining pet, soon becoming docile and friendly. It is light brown on the back with a pale stripe along each flank. The throat and underside are yellow. Though requiring a larger cage, its climatic requirements are similar to those described for Jones' Armadillo Lizard. It also is more omnivorous and may take soft fruit and canned dog food as well as the more usual invertebrate diet.

FAMILY LACERTIDAE—TYPICAL LIZARDS

With about 200 species in 22 genera, this family forms the "typical" lizards of Europe, Asia, and Africa. All are similar in general shape, with streamlined body, well-developed limbs, and a long, tapering tail.

European Green Lizard
Lacerta viridis

Length 40 cm (16 in). A native of central and southern Europe, this species will do well in captivity if given the right conditions. The male is bright green, developing tinges of blue in the breeding season. Females and youngsters are duller green, sometimes with a series of stripes along the body. It requires a large well-ventilated terrarium with air temperatures about 25°C (77°F) and a hotter basking area. Reduce

This is a young male Green Lizard, *Lacerta viridis.* Although frequently kept in Europe, this species seldom is available in the United States. Photo by R. D. Bartlett.

the temperature at night. It may be kept in an enclosed area outdoors in suitable climates. Feed it on large invertebrates, pinkie mice, and canned cat or dog food.

FAMILY TEIIDAE—TEGUS AND RACERUNNERS

Widely distributed from the USA through Central America to south-central Argentina and Chile, the teiids form a varied family with some 200 species in 40 genera. Many bear a superficial resemblance to lacertids, but there also are a few almost limbless, burrowing species.

Common Tegu
Tupinambis teguexin

Length: 120 cm (48 in). Tegus are perhaps the best known members of the family. The Common Tegu is native to tropical South America, where it occurs in a variety of habitats. This large, aggressive lizard, with its strong bite and sharp claws, is perhaps not suited for beginners, but it is an interesting subject for the more advanced herpetologist. The color is a glossy dark brown to black with numerous golden speckles. Tegus require a large, secure terrarium with firmly anchored furnishings, including a hollow log or hide-box and a large water bath. Maintain daytime temperatures in the region of 30°C (86°F), reduced to not less than 22°C (74°F) at night. Tegus are especially fond of snails, but also will take chicks, mice, lean minced meat, and raw eggs. A vitamin/mineral supplement should be regularly included in the diet.

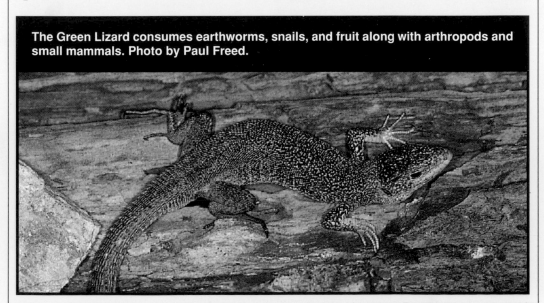

The Green Lizard consumes earthworms, snails, and fruit along with arthropods and small mammals. Photo by Paul Freed.

Captive-bred Gold Tegus, *Tupinambis teguixin,* tame more easily than wild-caught specimens. Photo by Isabelle Francais.